POISONOUS
SLOW LORISES

D1309577

Gareth Stevens
PUBLISHING

BY MARY MOLLY SHEA

Please visit our website, www.garethstevens.com. For a free color catalog of all our high-quality books, call toll free 1-800-542-2595 or fax 1-877-542-2596.

Cataloging-in-Publication Data

Names: Shea, Mary Molly.
Title: Poisonous slow lorises / Mary Molly Shea.
Description: New York : Gareth Stevens Publishing, 2018. | Series: Cutest animals...that could kill you!
| Includes index.
Identifiers: ISBN 9781538210956 (pbk.) | ISBN 9781538212721 (library bound) | ISBN 9781538210963
(6 pack)
Subjects: LCSH: Animal defenses–Juvenile literature. | Animal chemical defenses–Juvenile literature.
Classification: LCC QL759.B48 2018 | DDC 591.47–dc23

First Edition

Published in 2018 by
Gareth Stevens Publishing
111 East 14th Street, Suite 349
New York, NY 10003

Copyright © 2018 Gareth Stevens Publishing

Designer: Sarah Liddell
Editor: Therese Shea

Photo credits: Cover, p. 1 Seregraff/Shutterstock.com; wood texture used throughout Imageman/
Shutterstock.com; slash texture used throughout d1sk/Shutterstock.com; p. 4 Kasunhashanga/
Wikimedia Commons; p. 5 John Giustina/Photographer's Choice RF/Getty Images; pp. 7 (main),
11 warmer/Shutterstock.com; p. 7 (map) Adam Vilimek/Shutterstock.com; p. 9 Ch'ien Lee/Minden
Pictures/Minden Pictures/Getty Images; pp. 12–13 (python) Andrea Izzotti/Shutterstock.com;
pp. 12–13 (orangutan) KARI K/Shutterstock.com; p. 13 (slow loris) Hoang Mai Thach/Shutterstock.com;
p. 13 (hawk-eagle) MinhHue/Shutterstock.com; p. 14 Maky/Wikimedia Commons; p. 15 New York
Daily News Archive/Contributor/New York Daily News/Getty Images; p. 17 ZSSD/Minden Pictures/
Minden Pictures/Getty Images; p. 19 Praisaeng/Shutterstock.com; pp. 20–21 Barcroft Media/
Contributor/Barcroft Media/Getty Images.

Printed in China

CPSIA compliance information: Batch #CW18GS: For further information contact Gareth Stevens, New York, New York at 1-800-542-2595.

CONTENTS

Words in the glossary appear in **bold** type the first time they are used in the text.

ADORABLE LORISES

Have you ever heard of a loris? It's a big-eyed **primate**. It looks different from other primates, such as apes, chimpanzees, and people. It looks a bit like a strange stuffed animal!

Scientists think there are around eight species, or kinds, of lorises. Some species are called slow lorises. Even though they're just as cute as other lorises, be warned—they're poisonous! Read on to find out why you shouldn't even touch a slow loris.

SLENDER LORIS

THE DANGEROUS DETAILS

The slow loris is one of the only **mammals** in the world with a toxic bite!

SLOW LORISES HAVE SMALLER EYES THAN SLENDER LORISES. THEIR EYES ARE STILL PRETTY BIG, THOUGH!

SLOW LORIS

LOOKING FOR LORISES

Slow lorises are found in forests across southern Asia and parts of Southeast Asia. They're arboreal, which means they live in trees. They're active at night and sleep during the day.

Slow lorises have soft brown or gray fur and darker fur around their big eyes. They have small ears and no tail. They have short fingers, but can hang from branches by their feet. That leaves their hands free to **grab** things and eat!

THE DANGEROUS DETAILS

Lorises have very strong fingers and toes. They can hold onto branches with their hands or feet for really long periods of time.

SLOW LORISES ON THE MAP

ASIA

AUSTRALIA

WHERE SLOW LORISES LIVE

HOW SLOW?

Are slow lorises really slow? They're called slow lorises just because they usually move a bit slower than slender lorises. However, slow lorises can move fast and far if they have to. Some may travel 5 miles (8 km) a night searching for food. But slow lorises can remain still for hours if danger is nearby!

Slow lorises are omnivores. That means they eat many different kinds of things, including bugs, small animals, fruits, and plants.

THE DANGEROUS DETAILS

Slow lorises have a very long tongue for drinking **nectar** from flowering plants.

LONELY LORIS

Though a few slow lorises have been found living together, most live alone. They have their own territory in which to find food. Males usually have territories larger than females' territories. They mark their territory so others know to stay away. They do this with their pee!

Slow lorises put their pee on their hands. Then, they wipe it on branches for other animals to smell. Some scientists think the pee makes lorises' hands sticky so they can hang onto branches better.

THE DANGEROUS DETAILS
Slow lorises hiss and growl when they see an unwanted visitor.

PRIMATE PROTECTION

The largest slow lorises are only about 14.5 inches (37 cm) long. Some larger animals like to eat them. These include hawk-eagles, orangutans, and long snakes called pythons.

Slow lorises **protect** themselves in several ways. They may try to stay still and blend in with a tree. They may roll up, with their arms over their head and their back to the predator. They may even let go of a branch and fall to get away. If the predator bites a slow loris, it gets a surprise: poison!

ORANGUTAN

SLOW LORISES MAY BITE THEIR PREDATORS. THEIR BITE CAN BE POISONOUS, TOO.

PYTHON

HAWK-EAGLE

13

POISONOUS PRIMATE!

Slow lorises groom, or clean, their fur every day. They use their tongue and special front teeth, which are placed side by side like the teeth on a comb.

Slow lorises have **glands** that make poison near their elbows. When they groom themselves, they take the poison into their mouth and spread it over their fur. So, if a predator bites a loris, it's poisoned by the loris's fur. And if a slow loris bites a predator, the predator is poisoned by the loris's toxic mouth!

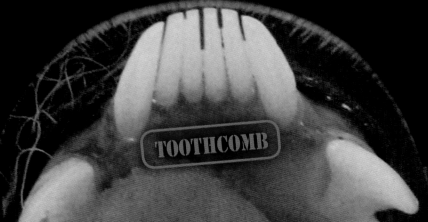

TOOTHCOMB

SLOW LORISES' SPECIAL FRONT
TEETH ARE CALLED A TOOTHCOMB.
THEY ALSO HAVE A SECOND TONGUE
FOR CLEANING THESE TEETH! YOU
CAN SEE IT IN THIS PHOTO.

SECOND TONGUE

TOXIC LORIS BABIES

Slow loris males and females come together to **mate** every 12 to 18 months. Females **whistle** to draw mates. About 6 months later, a female gives birth to one or two babies.

Mothers leave their babies in a nest to look for food. They give them a special way to protect themselves, though—their poison! Slow loris mothers groom their young. So, they put their own poison on the baby's fur. By the time slow lorises are 2, they're ready to leave and protect themselves.

THE DANGEROUS DETAILS

Slow loris babies make special high sounds to call their parents. People can't hear these sounds!

17

A DEADLY BITE

It's rare to see a slow loris and even rarer to be bitten by one. However, this does happen. People report that loris bites are very painful. One person even died from the poison.

In 2014, a scientist was bitten by a slow loris he had caught. His mouth swelled up, his chest and stomach hurt, and he had trouble breathing. His throat started to close up, too. Luckily, the scientist was close to a place where he could get **medicine**. It probably saved his life!

THE DANGEROUS DETAILS

The scientist said he has been bitten by many animals, but the slow loris's bite was the most painful of all.

THE SCIENTIST DIDN'T BLAME THE SLOW LORIS. IN FACT, HE SAID IT WAS TRYING TO HIDE FROM HIM.

19

PRIMATES IN PERIL

Slow lorises may be poisonous, but they still face many dangers. Their forest homes are knocked down for farms and buildings. People hunt them for food and medicine. They're also taken from the wild to become pets. Their teeth are removed, so they can't bite! One species is endangered, or in danger of dying out completely.

These cute primates need people's help to stay alive. Keep learning about them. Maybe you can be a scientist who helps slow lorises someday. Just don't get bitten!

THE JAVAN SLOW LORIS IS THE ONLY SLOW LORIS SPECIES BELIEVED TO BE ENDANGERED, BUT ALL SLOW LORIS SPECIES ARE **VULNERABLE** TO DYING OUT.

JAVAN SLOW LORIS

SUFFERING SLOW LORIS SPECIES

BENGAL SLOW LORIS
POPULATION: VULNERABLE

GREATER SLOW LORIS
POPULATION: VULNERABLE

JAVAN SLOW LORIS
POPULATION: **CRITICALLY** ENDANGERED

PHILIPPINE SLOW LORIS
POPULATION: VULNERABLE

PYGMY SLOW LORIS
POPULATION: VULNERABLE

GLOSSARY

critically: in great danger of happening

gland: a body part that makes something that is used by the body to function

grab: to quickly take and hold something with hands or arms

mammal: a type of animal that feeds milk to its young and that usually has hair or fur covering most of its skin

mate: to come together to make babies. Also, one of two animals that come together to make babies.

medicine: matter that is used in treating illness or pain

nectar: a sweet liquid made by plants

primate: any member of the group of animals that includes human beings, apes, and monkeys

protect: to guard from harm

vulnerable: open to harm

whistle: to make a high and loud sound by forcing air through lips or teeth

FOR MORE INFORMATION

BOOKS

Allgor, Marie. *Endangered Rain Forest Animals.* New York, NY: PowerKids Press, 2013.

Higgins, Nadia. *Deadly Adorable Animals.* Minneapolis, MN: Lerner Publications, 2013.

WEBSITES

15 Cute Animals That Could Kill You
www.mnn.com/earth-matters/animals/photos/15-cute-animals-that-could-kill-you/secret-weapon-cuteness
Discover more cute animals that could kill you!

Loris Facts
www.softschools.com/facts/animals/loris_facts/110/
Read about all kinds of lorises.

Loris Facts and Information for Kids
www.activewild.com/loris-facts-and-information-for-kids/
Find out more facts about these primates.

INDEX